All About Dirt Bikes:
a book for kids, by a kid!

By Carmine Q

DEDICATION

Thanks to my mom for helping me create this book, to my dad for always being willing to drive me to dirt bike tracks, to my brother for riding with me and to my dog for always being sweet. Thanks also to Eli Tomac, Deeo and Haiden "Danger Boy" Deegan for inspiring me to ride.

TABLE OF CONTENTS

Hi reader! Thanks for reading this book.
You'll notice some words throughout the book that are
highlighted in **bold**. The definition of these words
can be found in the very back of the book in
our glossary called "Words To Know".

We hope this book helps you learn all about dirt bikes…and
maybe some new vocabulary words too!
Enjoy and have fun!

1) WHAT IS A DIRT BIKE?

Dirt bikes are motorcycles that are specifically designed to go off-road. "Off-road" usually means areas that aren't covered with pavement or **asphalt** and instead are covered by natural materials such as dirt, gravel, mud or snow. Off-road areas can be found in many different places, including **recreation** areas that are designed for off-road equipment.

LevgenOnyshchenko©123RF.com

Dirt bikes aren't the only type of equipment that can be used off-road: other options can include All **Terrain** Vehicles (ATVs), mountain bikes and snowmobiles. However, in my opinion, dirt bikes are one of the most fun ways to enjoy off-road riding and can be safely used by kids of almost all ages.

2) DIRT BIKES VS. MOTORCYCLES

So what's the difference between a dirt bike and a motorcycle? There are a few important differences.

First, dirt bikes are designed to be lighter weight than a motorcycle that you would drive on the road. This allows a dirt bike rider to use the bike to perform cool tricks (more about tricks later) because it's easier to **maneuver** the bike while riding or jumping.

Next, dirt bikes are designed to have a higher clearance. "Clearance" means that the body of the dirt bike (where the engine is) is higher off the ground so that it can be ridden in areas that may have rocks, hills or other obstacles.

evrenkalinbacak©123RF.com

Finally, another important difference is in the tires. Dirt bikes have knobby tires, meaning the tires are bumpy, which allow the dirt bike to be ridden on natural materials like dirt, rocks and snow. Dirt bike tires provide better traction for the rider to ensure they are safe. Regular motorcycles usually have a smoother tire that is designed to be ridden on a road.

venerala©123RF.com

Did you know? Dirt bikes are made with either a "2-stroke" or a "4-stroke" engine. If you've ever heard a dirt bike make the famous "braaapp" sound, that's because it has a 2-stroke engine.

3) DIFFERENT STYLES OF RIDING DIRT BIKES

One of my favorite parts about dirt bikes is that there are so many different styles of riding, races and tracks. It's fun to check out videos of these different styles on YouTube and, if you're lucky, even attend a live event in the city or town where you live. Here are a few of the different styles:

- <u>Motocross</u>: This style is sometimes **abbreviated** as "MX". Motocross races happen outdoors. Many MX tracks include tight turns and high jumps. The width of the track is usually between 16 and 40 feet wide. The length is typically between ½ mile to 2 miles long.

parilovv©123RF.com

- Supercross: Supercross races are different from motocross primarily because Supercross races happen indoors. They are usually in a stadium or large arena - in fact, in some larger cities that have a football stadium Supercross races will be held at the same stadium. The organizers of the race will **haul** in dirt to create a Supercross track where football is usually played. Because Supercross races happen indoors, the tracks are sometimes narrower than in MX races.

evrenkalinbacak©123RF.com

- Endurocross: Endurocross, or enduro racing, is designed to test a rider's endurance. Having "endurance" as a dirt bike rider means that the rider has the strength to continue riding and finishing the race even if the rider feels tired or stressed out. Endurance is important for athletes in every sport, not just dirt biking. Enduro races are often longer than either MX or

Supercross events: they can last several hours. Enduro tracks also feature more obstacles, including large boulders, tree logs and high concrete **barriers**.

- <u>Freestyle</u>: Freestyle motocross, or FMX, is one of the most fun styles of riding to watch. Riders work hard to complete as many jumps and tricks as they can during the event. Extreme sports events like the X Games are where you can often see freestyle riding.

Gary Perkin©123RF.com

Did you know? MX and Supercross races are the most popular styles of dirt bike events in most areas. It's fun to attend both kinds of events; however, in an MX event you may only be able to see a small portion of the track (because it is outdoors) while at a Supercross event you can usually see the entire track at once (because you're sitting in a seat at a stadium or arena).

4) ALL ABOUT SAFETY

Before we talk about different types of dirt bikes and cool tricks that can be done on dirt bikes, we need to first talk about the most important **element** of riding dirt bikes: safety. Like many other sports, dirt biking can be very dangerous if you don't take the necessary safety **precautions**. Riding safely is important for riders of every age, including kids.

- Ride with an adult or, if you're an older kid, make sure an adult always knows where you're riding. If you get stuck or crash, it's important for an adult to be able to help you. If you're riding by yourself, make sure an adult knows when you will be back (ex. tell the adult "I'll be back in 20 minutes"): in case you don't come back in that timeframe then the adult will know to come find you.

- Make sure your dirt bike is the right size and power for your size and abilities. When you first start riding dirt bikes it can be **tempting** to ride a bike that's bigger than you need. Doing so can be very dangerous: if the bike is too big then you won't be able to safely get on and off the bike, and if it's too powerful then you may be more likely to ride too fast, get out of control or crash.

KonstatinPukhov©123RF.com

- Never ride a dirt bike on a paved street or road where there are cars or other vehicles. Not only is this usually illegal, it is extremely dangerous. Dirt bikes are designed to be ridden in off-road areas only. Some dirt bikes are called "dual-purpose", which means that they are designed to be ridden on paved roads as well as off-road: these types of bikes are for adults only.

5) ALL ABOUT GEAR

Mykhaylo Pelin©123RF.com

From your very first ride on a dirt bike, it is important that you have basic safety gear. You should never ride a dirt bike, even for a short distance, unless you have the following:

- Helmet
- Goggles
- Long sleeve shirt
- Long pants
- Sturdy boots that go up over your ankle (hiking boots can work well)
- Gloves

There is other gear that many riders will use that are "nice to have" but not necessarily required. This includes gear like a chest plate, neck protector and elbow pads/guards. Most beginning riders don't need to have these additional items to start riding dirt bikes but as you become a better (and faster!) rider you might want to invest in additional gear to help keep you safe.

If you buy all of this gear brand new at a motorcycle or sports store it can be very expensive. However, there is good news for beginning riders: you can often find used gear that is still in high-quality condition. I've bought a lot of my gear on social media sites like Facebook (always with my parents' help) where you can find groups **dedicated** to buying and selling motorcycles, dirt bikes and gear. eBay is another great place to search for used gear. I've even found some gear at garage sales!

Did you know? For many professional sports like football and soccer you can buy a jersey with your favorite player's name on it. That's not true for dirt biking: you can't buy jerseys with your favorite rider's name on it. I don't know why dirt biking is different from other sports but if you're looking for a rider's jersey you probably won't find it.

6) TYPES OF DIRT BIKES

Now that we've covered safety, let's get to the fun stuff. First, the different companies, styles and sizes of dirt bikes. Here's a list of some of the most popular companies which **manufacture** dirt bikes as well as their color(s): each company always makes their bike with that color(s) so you can easily **recognize** it when you see it on the track.

- KTM (orange)
- Yamaha (blue)
- Kawasaki (green)
- Honda (red)
- Husqvarna (blue and yellow)
- Suzuki (yellow)

ynos999©123RF.com

If you're just starting out riding dirt bikes, it's not important to have a favorite brand or company. However, if you follow professional riders, it is usually very easy to see which company (like KTM or Honda) **sponsors** them: they will be riding the latest version of the bike and will have the company's name and brand all over the bike and their gear.

Aleksandr Proshkin©123RF.com

Did you know? The colors on a Husqvarna dirt bike are blue and yellow because Husqvarna was originally a Swedish brand. The colors of the Sweden flag are blue and yellow.

7) DIRT BIKE ENGINES

I already mentioned that most dirt bikes have a 2-stroke or 4-stroke engine. The other way that dirt bike engines are identified is with a number of "cc"s. For example, a "Kawasaki KX85" model dirt bike means that the engine is an 85cc. A "Honda CRF250" model dirt bike means that the engine is a 250cc. But what does cc mean? The "cc" stands for cubic centimeters and is a measure of the size of the engine. Generally, the higher the cc, the more powerful the engine.

tarczas©123RF.com

Some people may think that the taller you are, the higher cc engine you should have: this is not true. Some adult-size bikes can have lower number cc engines while some kid-size bikes can have higher number cc engines

8) HOW TO SIZE YOUR DIRT BIKE

If you're a beginner rider, finding the right size dirt bike is very important. So how do you know if a bike is the right size?

One of the most important measurements is to sit on the bike and see where your feet touch the ground. If your feet don't touch then the bike is definitely too big. If your feet do touch, you want to be almost on your tippy-toes when both feet are on the ground: only the front part of your feet should touch and the heels of both feet should be off the ground. Another option is to ask someone at a motorcycle shop to help measure you: they are experts and even if you don't buy a new bike most people are usually happy to answer your questions (especially if you're a kid!)

scherbinator©123RF.com

The size of the bike's engine (remember those cc's?) is another **consideration** when buying a dirt bike. Although engine size is up to you (and your parents), beginning riders should start with a lower number cc engine. This allows riders to learn how to ride on a less powerful engine and will help you build confidence. Many kids' dirt bikes are built with a lower number cc engines so it will be easy to find one that's right for your skill level.

Did you know? Many motorcycle shops sell **replica** dirt bikes that are fun to play with. You can buy these toys to create a collection of your favorite dirt bike brands and styles. I like to use mine in our backyard: I build a mini track in the dirt (rocks and sticks make great obstacles for an enduro course!) and use my toy bikes to create races. Some stores may also sell other smaller accessories such as cool stickers and water bottles from popular gear brands like Fox Racing or Alpinestars. These are fun ways to show your love for dirt biking even when you're not riding.

9) CARE AND MAINTENANCE

Buying a dirt bike is a big **investment**: it's important to take care of your bike so that it runs safely and will be fun to ride for many years. Taking care of your bike is also one of the best ways to learn all the different parts of a motorcycle and how they work together. There are some basic maintenance items that you should do on a regular basis, including:

- Wash it! (but be gentle: you don't want to spray it with too much pressure and damage the engine, or spray water directly in areas of the engine that should remain dry)
- Inspect and clean the chain
- Check and clean the air filter
- Change the oil
- Check the tire pressure

Georgiy Datsenko©123RF.com

If you (or your parents) don't know how to do these things, don't worry! There are great videos available on YouTube that show you step-by-step instructions. Your local motorcycle shop is another good resource to help you get started. It may sound like a lot of work but maintaining your bike is an important part of being a responsible and safe rider.

10) TRICKS, TRICKS AND MORE TRICKS

Once you learn the basics of dirt biking, including how to ride safely, you will probably want to start learning to do tricks. Before you try any tricks, it is important that you can successfully land your bike after a jump. This means that you understand how to control and balance your dirt bike. This is a very important **foundation** to start from when learning tricks.

evrenkalinbacak©123RF.com

Here are some of the most popular tricks. It takes time and practice (lots of practice!) to be able to do these tricks well: if you need inspiration to keep trying to get it right, check out videos of your favorite professional riders to see how it's done.

crisagperez©123RF.com

- Wheelie: this trick can be practiced by beginners and professionals both, and involves riding on the back tire while your front tire is up off the ground

- Whip: a whip is when a rider jumps and pulls the dirt bike up **parallel** to the ground while it's in the air

davidherraez©123RF.com

- Can-can: a can-can is when a rider jumps and, while at the height of the jump, crosses one leg across the top of the seat with a straight leg

- No-legger: a no-legger is when a rider extends both legs straight out from the bike while in the air

- Flips: there are many different types of flips, including singles, doubles, back flips and even a super-duper advanced flip called the "heart attack"

- 360: the 360 trick is just what it sounds like: turning your bike around in a full circle (360 degrees) while in the air

- Heel-clicker: a heel-clicker is a difficult trick where the rider lifts both legs and puts them in front of the handle bars while touching the heels of his feet together, all while jumping the bike

Did you know? Professional dirt bike and stunt rider Robbie Madison rode his dirt bike across water in 2017. He reached a speed of 35 MPH while riding the waves in Tahiti, an island in the South Pacific. You can find the incredible video of his trick on YouTube….just make sure you don't try it at home!

homy_design©123RF.com

11) PARTS OF A DIRT BIKE TRACK

If you've ever seen a dirt bike track you may not realize that each section of the track has a specific name. A track is made up of more than just random bumps and jumps - track designers work hard to create a track that is challenging for the riders. Some of the key parts of most dirt bike tracks include:

federicorostagno©123RF.com

- Berm: a berm is an area where the dirt has been piled up and packed down to allow for riders to take a turn in the track

- Whoops: whoops are **continuous** bumps that are small enough for riders to skim over without having to jump

- Double jump: a double jump, also known as a "jump to jump", is 2 jumps in a row where the rider rides up one jump, jumps across to the 2nd jump and comes down on the far side of the 2nd jump

Mykhaylo Pelin©123RF.com

- Triple jump: like a double jump but a triple jump is 3 jumps in a row

- Tabletop jump: a tabletop jump is like a double jump where there is dirt filled in between the jumps (creating a "tabletop" flat surface between both jumps)

- Rhythm section: a series of continuous jumps (higher than whoops) where riders will jump over 2 or 3 jumps at a time

Did you know? The dirt used to create a track can be different depending on where you live in the U.S.A. Dirt, also known as "soil", can have very different texture and consistency from state to state. Areas like southern California often have a clay-based soil which can be very hard (it feels like dried up Playdoh). Tracks in states like Nevada might have soil that is sandier. Areas like Colorado typically have soil that is more like what you might find in a garden. The type of dirt on a track or even in a recreational area can impact your riding so make sure you know what you're riding on and take extra precautions to be safe.

12) FAMOUS RIDERS - ADULTS

Dirt biking is popular in many parts of the world and you can find professional riders from many different countries. Here are some of my favorite professional riders from the U.S.A. as well as other countries:

- Eli Tomac: Tomac is an American professional motocross and supercross racer from Colorado. He was born in 1992. He currently races for the Kawasaki racing team. He is the son of professional motocross and BMX racer John Tomac. He has won numerous events in the Monster Energy AMA Supercross racing series and has ridden on tracks across the U.S.A.

- Ryan Dungey: Dungey is an American professional motocross and supercross racer from Minnesota. He was born in 1989. In 2018 he officially retired from professional racing. During his career he raced for the Suzuki and KTM teams. Before his retirement he won many U.S. and international races, including AMA motocross and supercross as well as the "Motocross des Nations", the world's largest international race.

- Ashley Fiolek: Fiolek is an American professional motocross racer from Michigan. She was born in 1990. Fiolek was born deaf which is one of the reasons why she began racing dirt bikes: she could do it herself and didn't have to listen or talk to anyone else during a race. When Fiolek turned 21 she retired from professional racing and now coaches younger riders.

- Ricky Carmichael: Carmichael is an American professional supercross racer from Florida. He was born in 1979. He is known for winning multiple championships in races during the 2000s. He has won so many times that he is known as the "GOAT", the Greatest Of All Time. He also races stock cars, winning races at speedways across the U.S.A. Carmichael is also a sports broadcaster for Monster Energy AMA Supercross races.

- Ken Roczen: Roczen is a German professional motocross and supercross racer. He was born in 1994. Although he is from Germany, he is well known in the U.S.A. for winning many AMA supercross as well as motocross races. He has also won the international Motocross des Nations race. He currently rides for Honda's HRC (Honda Racing Corporation) team.

Did you know? Although dirt biking is fun for everyone, there are usually more men and boys who ride than women and girls. One girl is trying to change that trend: 12-year old Tanya Muzinda is from Mozambique (a country on the continent of Africa) and she loves riding dirt bikes. Tanya is helping people to see that both boys and girls can be successful riders and that anyone can learn to ride. Check out videos of Tanya on YouTube for more information.

---

13) FAMOUS RIDERS – KIDS/TEENS

There are a lot of great younger riders who are technically **amateurs** but are still fun to watch and follow. The best young riders are already sponsored by dirt bike companies and gear brands and they travel to races across the U.S.A. Here are some of my favorite amateur riders:

- Haiden "Danger Boy" Deegan: Deegan was born in 2006 and is from Temecula, CA. He is one of the most famous young dirt bike riders thanks to his "Danger Boy" nickname. Deegan has won more than 30 championship and became the youngest rider ever to successfully land a backflip when he was 10 years old. His dad is Brian Deegan, a famous motocross rider.

- Jett Reynolds: Reynolds was born in 2004 and is from Bakersfield, CA. He currently rides for Kawasaki. He has won the "youth racer of the year" award several times.

- Daxton Bennick: Bennick was born in 2006 and is from South Carolina. He currently rides for KTM's "Orange Brigade" team. He has 3 titles from the Loretta Lynn AMA race as well as 30 national titles.

Russell Ensley©123RF.com

Did you know? Because the best amateur youth riders compete in races across the country, they don't usually attend a regular school with other kids. Instead they are homeschooled. This allows them to keep up with their studies and still do what they love: dirt biking!

14) FAMOUS TRACKS IN THE U.S.A.

Most states in the U.S.A. have great MX tracks available for professional and amateur riders. States like California, Arizona, Texas and Florida have many tracks because of the warm weather and ability to ride year-round. However, don't worry if you live in a different state: places like Colorado, Michigan and New Jersey also have great tracks.

Many dirt bike tracks are locally owned and are often a family-run business. It's fun to get to know the owners of the track: you can learn more about how the track started, how they decide on the design of the track and what plans they might have to add additional tracks in the future.

Most tracks also have a social media page: follow their page to make sure you know when the track is open, especially if it's been raining or snowing. There's nothing worse than getting excited about riding your dirt bike, driving to the track and then discovering that it's closed because of weather or poor track conditions.

15) OTHER COOL STUFF

These are a few other things about dirt bikes that I learned when I started riding and I thought you might want to know them too:

- Graphics kits: Did you know you can customize your bike with a personalized graphics kit? These kits include decals that you can stick on the plastic parts of most dirt bikes. I was able to create a cool custom front plate that includes my name, number and some of my most favorite company logos like GoPro, Fox and Kawasaki.

- Accessories: Another cool way to personalize your bike is with accessories. Many motorcycle stores will sell accessories like hand guards, handlebars and exhaust pipes. These accessories can make your dirt bike look like it was made just for you.

- Video games: Of course, it's always more fun to be riding dirt bikes in real life, but if the weather is bad or you just can't get to the track, there are a few fun dirt bike video games. I really like to play Monster Energy Supercross or MXGP 2019. Both games are great because you can play with your friends. You can also design your own track which is fun.

16) WORDS TO KNOW

- Abbreviated: making a word shorter or briefer

- Amateur: a person who rides for sport or fun rather than as a professional career

- Asphalt: a mixture of substances used for paving roads

- Barriers: an obstacle; a limit or boundary of any kind

- Consideration: a careful thought; something to be kept in mind while making a decision

- Continuous: uninterrupted

- Dedicated: being committed to something

- Element: a component or part of a whole

- Foundation: the basis or groundwork of anything

- Haul: to carry or transport

- Investment: to spend money on something

- Maneuver: to change the position of something

- Manufacture: to make or produce something

- Parallel: extending in the same direction and never crossing

- Precautions: measures taken in advance to prevent danger or injury

- Recognize: to identify something or someone

- Recreation: a pastime that provides relaxation and enjoyment

- Replica: a close or exact copy of something

- Sponsors: a company who provides free products or services to someone, usually in exchange for that person representing the company in public

- Tempting: enticing or inviting

- Terrain: a tract of land with reference to its natural characteristics (e.g. the rocky terrain)

- Traction: the adhesive friction of something on a surface (e.g. a tire on a road)

ACTIVITIES!

I hope you enjoy creating your own artwork on the coloring pages and solving the dirt bike-themed crossword and word search puzzles. Have fun!

Artwork credit: http://minarium.club/full/

Artwork credit: https://www.sembagine.com/dirt-bike-coloring-sheets-printable/

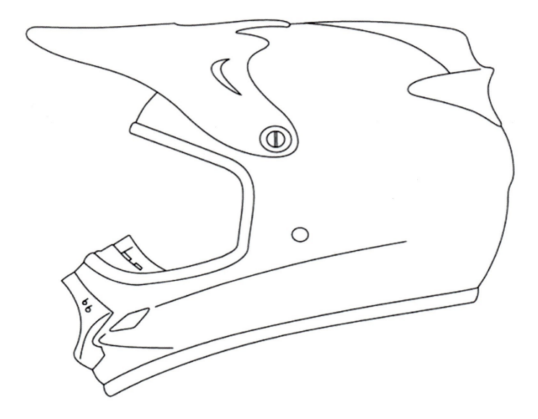

Artwork credit: https://paintingvalley.com/motocross-helmet-drawing

WORD LIST:

DIRTBIKE
ENDURO
ENGINE
GOGGLES
GRAPHICS
HELMET
HONDA
JUMPS
KAWASAKI
KTM
MOTOCROSS
OFFROAD
SAFETY
SUPERCROSS
WHIP
WHOOPS
YAMAHA

```
                Y  M  G  T  H
             B  T  P  O  L  E  O  E  G
          V  S  U  M  K  W  M  N  M  N  M
       H  S  P  O  O  H  W  L  D  K  H  S  E
       P  S  T  M  F  C  Y  E  A  T  D  S  K
    J  Y  O  K  O  Y  F  F  H  E  M  U  O  I  I
    Y  Y  R  A  R  A  S  R  N  H  P  G  Z  B  C
    A  T  C  W  U  E  N  I  O  E  R  G  R  T  K
    X  E  O  A  D  F  G  I  R  A  S  O  W  R  F
    S  F  T  S  N  N  Z  C  P  P  D  G  H  I  T
       A  O  A  E  Y  R  H  M  Z  I  G  I  D
       S  M  K  E  O  I  U  A  O  X  L  P  O
          X  I  S  C  J  N  M  W  M  E  C
             S  S  A  H  A  M  A  Y  S
                B  M  J  Y  L
```

Word search made with www.mywordsearch.com

Across

2 This dirt bike company always uses the color orange.

7 Important gear to protect your eyes.

9 A style of dirt bike race that is held outdoors.

10 This trick happens when the rider makes the bike parallel to the ground.

13 A style of dirt bike race that features obstacles.

15 This dirt bike company always uses the color green.

17 In dirt bikes this is a 2-stroke or 4-stroke.

18 This dirt bike company always uses the color blue.

19 This is the most important aspect of riding dirt bikes.

Down

1 An area of dirt on a track that is packed down and helps the riders to make turns.

3 This type of jump is featured in many dirt bike tracks.

4 Dirt bikes are just 1 type of this 2-wheeled vehicle.

5 This trick has a lot of different versions and should only be performed by professional riders.

6 Important gear to protect your head.

8 These kits are a cool way to customize your dirt bike.

11 A feature of dirt bike tracks with continuous small bumps.

12 This dirt bike company always uses the colors blue and yellow.

14 This dirt bike company always uses the color red.

16 This trick happens when your front wheel comes up off the ground.

WORD LIST:

BERM	GRAPHICS	KTM	WHEELIE
ENDUROCROSS	HELMET	MOTOCROSS	WHIP
ENGINE	HONDA	MOTORCYCLE	WHOOPS
FLIPS	HUSQVARNA	SAFETY	YAMAHA
GOGGLES	KAWASAKI	TABLETOP	

ABOUT THE AUTHOR

I was born in 2008 and I love dirt bikes. I currently ride a Kawasaki KLX140 but have also ridden a Yamaha TTR125 and a Kawasaki KLX110. I live near Denver, Colorado and am lucky to be able to ride with my friends at several tracks in the area, including Watkins Motocross, IMI Motorsports Complex and Thunder Valley. I also love checking out new bikes and gear at Performance Cycle and Fay Myers. When I'm not ripping up the pro tracks, I am focused on doing well at school and spending time with my family and our miniature poodle named Marlin.

Why did I write this book?
When I first started dirt biking, I couldn't wait to find some books to help me learn all about my new hobby. Unfortunately, I couldn't find anything, so I decided to write one myself. I hope this book will help other kids learn about dirt biking (and maybe their parents too!)

Made in the USA
Middletown, DE
05 November 2023

41984502R00029